ENCOURAGING SHAKESPEARE

Encouraging Shakespeare

ROBERT HULL

PETERLOO POETS

First published in 1993
by Peterloo Poets
2 Kelly Gardens, Calstock, Cornwall PL18 9SA, U.K.

**A catalogue record for this book is available
from the British Library**

ISBN 1-871471-32-X

Printed in Great Britain by
Latimer Trend & Company Ltd, Plymouth

ACKNOWLEDGEMENTS are due to the editors of *Cumberland Poetry Review* (USA) and *Poetry Matters* in whose pages some of these poems first appeared.

Five of the poems in this volume appeared in *Peterloo Preview 2* (1990).

This volume was published with assistance from the Ralph Lewis Award at the University of Sussex.

Supported by

Cornwall
County Council

Contents

New Reading Glasses

Rational friend and lover
of things as they are,

you arrest my recent retreat
from too much raw nearness.

I re-acknowledge the drab assurance
of door-keys, timetables.

I'm freshly deferential
in the accomplished presences

of print, pictures.
Backing off from menus

with the movements
of an uncertain trombonist

or as if adjusting
a personal stereoscope

may no longer be necessary,
but addressing ordinary

Lilliputian presumptions
I lose the certain

benefits of confusion.
As to whether notices say anything,

and whether the ear-ring
lying on the table is or

is not a sardine-can-opener.
That satisfactory scattering

of vagueness settled
on all things close

has gone. I want the kerbful
of dandelions

to be a choir in saffron again,
the phone book

to have a million
numbers all the same.

Hands

Folded
and finished
seven years ago.

Remembered
in football crowds,
crossing roads.

I see them
driving your old Rover,
in the next room

writing, reaching
to welcome me home. Seven
years ago today

they held a racket,
cut flowers,
wrote me a letter,

and carrying a tray up
late at night
clutched at the stairs.

Axe

You wouldn't have left it out
inviting comparisons,

though gathering dew
overnight

probably suited it
better than yesterday's

ill-timed fit
of being wielded

on jarring heart-wood
and let skid

vertiginously
off missed edges.

Now I can't wrestle it
out of an obstinate

refusal to resume,
it won't (head hunched

in the block's
grip) relinquish

its tenacious
inertia.

From a distance
it has the posture

of The Thinker —
wondering what

it might next be hurled at,
grimly nostalgic

for the better-
aimed sort of life

it once had
with you, father.

Village

Somewhere near here, each Sunday,
a lift from Mr Rigby
in his milk-float.

It was pleasant
being trotted home from church,
one foot

on the cart step swaying,
the air cold as a wheel-rim.
At school we leaned through railings

hearing old women's talk,
and watching wagons being shunted
under sun-filled smoke,

the strays riding free,
brake-handles clanging.
They've taken the wall-top tiles away

that burnt our bare-legged shin-over
to be first home,
and where the old line ran,

dragonflies make timeless halts
on the stopped air.
No Coffee Days now,

no trombones, banners, horses,
no rector
waving a wild bat.

Rectory Close
resounds with small mowers,
where there were rooks at dusk,

the old men's careful dialect,
the slow tiff of bowls.
A relinquishable place —

except for fragments of you
I keep finding:
some Home-Guard gear,

a few letters,
your old speed-skates
piled in a wardrobe.

The Graveyard by Croston Church School

Bury me here
By Yarrow River,
near the wooden bridge
the children skip over;
bury me here
where the river goes under.

Bury me here
where their voices shriek
across the churchyard
five days a week;
bury me here
near schoolroom clamour.

Bury me here
where waiting mums
gossip and peer
into each others' prams;
bury me here
where I'm part of a future.

Bury me here
where the pavingstones
on this glistening path
are old gravestones;
bury me here
for the rain to walk over.

Bury me here
where flowers are tended,
where little is said
and no grief mended;
bury me here
where the love-lorn linger.

Bury me here
under the bells
that fall to quiet
as the church fills;
bury me here
when the ringing's over.

Bury me here
where I was born,
near silent orchards
and ripening corn.
Bury me here
in a quiet corner.

For the Child Who Became Christopher

May you come safe
        and flawless

May they gaze in awe
            at your small creased wrists
            and marvel
                at your perfect breath
                    and ordinariness

May they gurgle at you
        and drool gratitude

May your gaze and grip
        reassure them

May your limbs
        be proper and deft
            your crawl furious
                your falls neat

May your most frightening dark
            be in stories
            the deepest thunder
            over the hills yonder

May no-one fence you round
        with their own hopes
            or shawl you in their dreams

May your teachers learn
        from your crazes
            and amazements

May your friends
        be a bridge to cross over
            in any weather

May you have without too much wanting
   and want without too much need

May there be sacred places
   to return to

May stones fall short
   and only low branches break
    and swings miss you
       on the way back.

Exploratory

Even before you went in
I think there was something in you
planning two small snowmen
next Sunday.

Quite sneakily
you didn't let on
to the honest white surgeon
—or the family—that your body

had no intention
of being intruded on for long,
and wouldn't really be needing
the flowers, the phone-calls,

the prayers,
the intercession
of any distant anxiety—
however welcome as courtesy.

I think that in general
it wouldn't pay anyone to want
you for a real patient.
You've too many unremovable

things like snow-men in your head,
so much stuff up your sleeve
that's more or less impossible
to locate or handle; I'd

say you were the last person
any operation not quite certain
of itself should approach.
I can imagine most pain

fading quietly away
to escape the disdain
of being greeted like the wrong visitor
arriving at the wrong time.

Any heaped-up white surgeon
would feel as frail as a snowman
if he knew the unforeseen condition of woman
he was called to perform on.

Someone might find listening
to your heart-beat more than enough
for theirs. And imagine trying
to sterilise that laugh.

Inheritance

The pearls, her father's watch,
the Victorian lace Christening dress,
some weighty linen—
things for the cool drawer
of another century.

The stale cushion-covers,
untouched home-made jams,
cards and pension books
go without much more grief
into black bin-liners.

As for the unsuspected curios—
we already show people the ancient
negatives, a fifty-year-old tin
of new 'Songster' gramophone needles,
a Valentine from the nineties.

But there are objects with memories
we're less sure what to do with:
some seventy-eights in covers,
the piano-music she played from,
two paint-boxes, with brushes.

And something like guilt stabs
at us, finding in her diary
the labour of its shaky
entries, the distress of a last
cheque-book's few scrawled stubs.

Return

Nil by mouth
last night. This morning,
the earth coming back.

The voice is a shock,
but how quickly
you're catching up with us,

trying some coffee,
saying you're watching magpies
in the sunlit oak

outside your room.
Perhaps by late afternoon
you'll wake less uncertainly,

follow the shadows
of the oak arranging dusk
in your room, hear the owl

try the slow
drip of its drawn-out call
down the dark woodland,

welcoming you back.

Moving

Along this passageway I've twice come
    carrying a week-old child.
Up these steps you've climbed
    again and again with burdens.
On these tiles a rag negro doll
    lay in the rain for days.
Through this window the September moonrise
    was familiar, unrhetorical.
These door-knobs have turned under our hands
    at all hours.
This fire has burned for us through our winters
    and ill weathers.
At this window faces waited.
On this hearth books lay.
These are the fences we neglected.
These are the doors we slammed.

Commerce

There are people who teach you
as you buy.

There was Tom Judd
who'd talk about engines and cars
till his profit ran dry.

And the man who showed me
not just binoculars
but a sky.

And others,
true educators
from whom we learn

matter-of-factness,
the syntax
of things as they are:

a grammar of mowers,
declensions of stars.

Encouraging Shakespeare

Murder most foul
of Macbeth it was.
It was no owl shrieked when Ross
the short-of-sight

entered at a fall
on his face,
sword twisted somewhere
unforgettable.

No thanes in history
despatched their thrice-
noble lines nightly
topped up with such foaming cruelty,

no Seyton as lily-livered
as I was cowered
in the wings waiting
for another helmet to roll,

praying that the forthcoming
demise of his gentle mistress
might be accomplished
without more gormless

scarfed-up laughter
from doubling kern or gallowglass
trying to keep a taut face.
Never such pillage

of syllable, such resolute
unseaming of metre;
never in Polanski, Hall or Nunn,
such amazing mayhem

—as when that fateful dagger
of the mind hovering
on hopefully the backcloth
was thrust quivering

between Macbeth's moonlit
shoulder-blades while he
soliloquised he saw it
still before him.

And yet, than in our true tragedy
where did ever audience
see comic relief as regularly
sweep in like the cavalry?

Where were players so well prepared
to put the bard to the sword?
When was vaulting ambition
so briskly interred?

Murders have been performed
too terrible for the ear
before ours, and will be hereafter,
but will Shakespeare,

cribbed, cabin'd and confounded
in death's dead audience
ever as nearly cry out,
'What bloody play was that?'

Columbus

'Generally it was my wish to pass no island without taking possession of it.'

The slaves were not profitable
'for almost half of them died'

but there were spears to be had
for broken crockery

and untouched rings of islets
like trinkets.

And though the Great Khan
finally went missing

and the gold pagodas
faded with the mists

there was the first flamingo
pink as dawn

there was the terminal innocence
of rivers.

When enough naked harbours
had been manacled

enough grief
requisitioned

a cargo of fables
set out for Spain, heavy

with lilting names —
Cathay   Indies

conquistadores   spices
syphilis.

Trip to Albania

In Albania
a woman in colourful peasant dress
is happily spinning

at the edge of a lake.
Another
is happily holding something

wooden and folk-loric.
The day-trip also promises
the view panoramic

with remarkable luncheon.
We have foregone
such frisson

in favour of studying
through shocked binoculars
idyllic shores

without people,
a harbour without boats,
the net curtains of khaki flats —

a stasis of streets
in a place where nobody
makes trips.

Akhmatova

They read you in secret,
ditched you in public;
there was 'nothing about the collective,
nothing except love'.

You harmed the young,
consorting with birdsong
and forest berries;
you displayed leanings towards empty

a-political skies.
Later they found it confusing
it was Akhmatova who stayed
to listen to a city's

anguished breathing
in streets where the rain
memorised you.
Your poems were passed

from silence to silence,
going into regions
ignorant of the place of words
in the work plan,

travelling without papers
beyond the last forest
to speak even in the camps.
Your readers return openly

to the streets now,
mixing freely with those
who would still silence you
and somewhere the few

who heard in mid-winter's
deserted air the name
'Akhmatova' ring
like an axe in a clearing.

Larkin

Like cloud shadow today
your death making its way

across England, across its towns,
counties, fields, lanes.

Slowly over cranes and spires,
and neglected waters,

along quiet branch-lines,
and college lawns

like cloud shadow it passes,
darkening recreation grounds,

estates with washing,
and slow widening

rivers. And you, going
ahead, at summer's pace cycling

down one of the lost lanes
at the end of the fens,

listening already
to oblivion whispering

from dusty stillnesses
where flowering grasses

hide the place-names.
In one of those faded Junes

you found somewhere
the start of a war —

queues of men, grinning
as if they were on the winning

side already,
the innocently

lived years ending
in spendthrift gesture.

Few such poems, all too few,
but no-one reproaches you

with this last silence,
though perhaps it means

you've let the literateurs
loose round canals and choirs

to finally hunt you down.
But you'll be left decently alone

by the less well read
your compassion celebrated —

those being pushed to the side
of their own lives,

or adrift between garish wedding
and drab bed-sitter.

They'd be the best people
to come forward —

though they might never have heard
of you, it's they who could

best speak in your memory
their own felt testimony,

like an awkward 'Here endeth'
pronounced quite loudly enough.

Hulot

saying
a bag in each hand
Hulot
a pipe in his mouth

Hulot

plasters Brittany
with misfires

on the spur of the moment
joins funerals

is chased by dogs into a dark
that erupts fireworks

Hulot

demolishes
any placid hotels
we have left in us

leaves wet footprints
in our heads

invisible
in his stopped motor
extends an arm
to caress a dog
whose tail knows it is

Hulot.

Cooper

Before you started
we laughed

so you stopped
while your hair

looked round
for moral support.

As we do now
for the fez

that was
the phizz

that went
just like that.

Meanwhile
egg bag

bag egg
and broken plates

falling
in helpless gratitude.

Another Butcher Poem

'How the customers laugh' — Craig Raine in *The Penguin Book of British Contemporary Poetry*.

'His face is hurt by the parting sinews' — Hugo Williams in the same volume.

In the shop I visit
the butcher frequently
carves all manner of meat
unemotionally,

with no evident anxiety,
and those who watch him
do so rather quietly,
with no-body falling about.

I've started to observe him
since butcher poems
appeared in the shops,
and judging from his demeanour,

for instance as he goes
in and out of the deep freeze,
it seems likely he sees
very little in there

worth writing home about.
He doesn't wince
at the nastier cuts. Mince
is mince, chump-end

and chine
come all the same;
he even makes most offal
seem quite possible.

I do suspect him though
of exactly measured distastes
for some of his customers.
His well-bred smile can truss and skewer

the best-heeled impatience,
and an immaculate reserve
lays out certain voices
in neat thin slices.

But that is about all
there seems to be to say about Mr Earley,
despite the contemporary
relevance of the poem

about butchers, like those
in this anthology that cost
me the price of about
four lamb chops.

In fact butchers is a subject
I'm as much roused by
as that pheasant is by the blue sky
his feet are hanging from.

Though his wife, I might add
—it could be good for trade—
grows lovely raspberries
and loganberries, and various

vegetables, which they sell
dirt cheap.
(Of course the general emphasis
remains on meat.)

A Case for Burning Books

'The world is everything that is the case.' — L. Wittgenstein

Them, or me. This room, amicably shared
once, grows tight-shelved, anonymous.
A week ago I finally sent bickering

on its way four foot of the lit. crit.
that was billeted on me in the seventies
as part of the late degree effort,

and since then I've shed a kilo or two
of successful contemporary fiction
and a pannierful of travel writing.

Education's under threat now;
found sanity can't offer house-room
to urgent works on curriculum reform

or journals of reading research
I can't even read slowly. Which is why
in the garden this morning I'm turning

various pages with a languid
foot, studying for the first time
passages from the most definitively

useless texts as they slowly
incinerate. I intend farewell next,
in even-handedness, to some rather whining

poetry (a book on The Third World mainly
but written in the first, another
all travel in Italy tra-la,

and one with clear views of dissidents
taken from unincarcerated distances).
Farewell soon, too, amongst others

less well noted, to Wittgenstein's
slightly whacky *Tractatus*, a volume which
I never learned to love or even confidently

pronounce — does it rhyme 'tomat-oes' or 'ate
us'? — to whom dying, though, I'll owe knowing
the world was everything that was the case.

But now that everything in this
case is for another world, I know
that each trip makes it more likely

you might eventually be paid the respect
due to you, Quixote, and I might soon know
wherever it is, wandering Herodotus, you've got to.

Molesworth 1, we'll have earlier sightings
of each other now, and young Pliny, you may even
get a reply soon to one of your letters,

now that these shelves are well rid
of so much that could never be well read,
and so much that began to be too much

for any relationship — ours having only received,
I hope, one of those sharp peremptory reviews
one accepts in time as being rather well considered.

The Painting on the Cover of our
LEAP Writing Magazine

which is no longer a painting
being shrunk and black
like something on a pole
out of *Heart of Darkness* by J. Conrad
was by Edvard (with a v) Munch
(the 'ch' as in 'sunk',
the 'u' as in Peter Sellers saying
'Clousot') called 'The Scream' (I think).

Whether it's a primal or personal or pathological
or (as on writing courses) partly
at least parturitional Scream
one can't tell.

We can see
it takes place at the end of a pier
(or tether)
and seems to be the concentrated
essence and sum of scream
representing
apparently at the sea-side
some sort of ultimate crunch
in the life of Edvard Munch;

which may have occurred
simply because there is much to scream about
in Norway like long dark nights with Ibsen
cross-country ski-ing
endless herring
and too many fjords.

But what is there we ask
similarly scream-inspiring
up the Institute
where this echo has taken residence
on our cover.

The local artist
who has skilfully located Munch-angst
in the centre of our musings
may have a point;
perhaps his screamer's
pelting down the pier
of a secure self
yelling an inaudible yell
before risking another terminal
LEAP
off who
they thought they were last week.

LEAP, the name of the course, is an acronym—
Literature as Expressive Art Product & Process.

Leader

He found harbours
for their exhaustions

and made firm roofs
for their songs.

He bound the pages
of their imagining

and illuminated
the hours of their day

with plainness.
When raids came

they battled
for their own snowfalls

and forests with eagles
and steaming byres

and the rough speech
that had kept vigil.

Reassurance by Tadpole

You called them Chernopoles,
they were so big;
and there'd been an east wind
and it had rained.

Still, they looked fine:
a scatter of blips as neat
as apostrophes, parked
on the white cliff-rise

up from the pond,
free to try out a second
element or flip
back to the first.

An easy Eden,
and from brawling spasm
to brink of diaspora
a routine

metamorphosis.
No need to wash the grass,
or rinse the rockery,
they can simply

go. We watch them
plink purposefully forward,
greatly re-assured.
They've come to no harm,

these sprightly Chernopoles;
they might even be jauntier
by a roentgen, brisker
for the extra bequerels.

Nearly Working

Riddance on it.
The morning's for watching the cat

watch a crow
sidle nervously up to the bacon.

It's for having no quarrel
with the local school bell

or even some farm machinery
grinding past dustily.

It's for acres of larks
ebbing upwards

to silence,
and inches of stir

under inert greenery.
It's for small figs

to grow green
and stolid in

and irises to tremble
and brandish wingy

flagrances of purple
strong enough

—it seems—to send the blackbird off
to tut-tut in the chestnut.

It's to kneel for the newt
with the spread hands

who banks down through weed
and sun turning to me

undersides
all yellow.

Gnome's Tale

Now I lie face down
with an arm gone.

I was fifth from left
in the seventh row.

I watched her enter,
consider the wrapped herons

a moment, and walk outside.
The drowsing white

carp would please her,
or the terracotta containers

for lobelias.
But neither those

nor any coloured
singing bird

was what she wanted.
Instead she paused

in front of us,
and before every

accomplished pixy,
fey wheelbarrow

and ever-grazing duck,
chose me.

She gave me a lake
to gaze across,

and woodland to guard.
She made me sole keeper

of all the fish
that lift to the light

and drift downwards.
She appointed me

official listener
to all the grass.

I had a position
near her words,

and heard her pleasure
in the darkness

as her movement woke
the scent of flowers.

I intended her to know
my loyalty,

my steadfast gratitude
for all this.

I would not flinch
from weather.

She would see how year
in year out

I would not tilt an inch
from true.

Frogs

Stone-grey
they come back
in grey February

to flounder in love
like the rest of us,
and writhe desperately,

and flop and grunt
and discard galaxies
of off-spring.

A precarious
dispersal
into dark grass

stops the mowing,
and farthing-
sized things

try the kitchen,
or the first rung
of a ten-

foot ladder,
or sway like stranded
pole-vaulters

on the tips
of grass-blades.
By mid-summer

the elders
are a glossy
green henge

of still heads,
angled skywards
like the corners

of foundered
crisp bags.
There's comedy

in their inert
sprawl hammocked
on pondweed,

algae draping
an eye, and
when they see

us move
and shoulder
their way under.

But in October
they fling themselves
across wet roads

at night after
trees have fallen,
and travel

to wintry stillness
under bricks
and stored wood.

Before I greet
next February's
chill survivals

I'll glimpse
legs trailing
under soaked logs,

find exhibits
of skin — green
and moist,

hunched
in a nimbus
of mould,

or drily
stretched out flat
in mid-flight.

Flood Pastoral

A small valley
thumped by a wind,

the path a clear blue trickle
that cleans the grass.

It's glittery February
rich in ditches,

and the river is backing
into a field

of snowdrops that hang
their heads under

or turn with the drifting
floodwater

or let the wind
have them.

The weir
overburdened

seems to be full of swans
trying to take off.

Youth

We left your scarf there
near the stone slipway somewhere,
amongst the gulls and rising water.

We went carelessly, leaving it
with the wind and light that day,
and the leaning grass and the clouds,

as if we thought we could easily
go back some other time to find
the black-headed gulls

printing the air with harsh cries,
the reeds and the shadows,
the lanes adrift in summer,

the water and the bird-calls
the leaning grass and the clouds
that the tide was taking.

Seaweed

This seaweed
swaying in clear water
under the harbour wall
I stare down from

is restless
with human gestures
reaching out hands
in profuse greeting

proffering elaborate thanks
then straining for
effect and floundering
in mid-gesture,

or it looks easy
as after a few drinks
and lifts itself
towards the surface

gathering from deep
somewhere a passionate
slow blue flamy light
that travels each frond

and fades at the point
like someone always
almost saying
something but knowing

each rising wave
of feeling dissipated
in gestures that cannot
complete themselves.

Word Watching

Along the river this morning
we've scrutinised obscure reeds
and choked weirs and tipped an eye
to the hospitable blue sky.

In our avid binoculars ditches
and distances have trembled
at each stop and search for species;
we've thumbed and thumbed the names

of various fleeting certainties
about this flower and that bird,
and not for a moment incurred
any risk of over-familiarity.

The morning has been charming.
In its early haze one of us flattered
some low-flying pheasants with — 'lapwings!',
and there have been several sightings

since then of the phrase 'reed warbler',
as continuously in and out of our talk
along the thick banks of the river
'redshank', 'blackcap' and 'snipe'

have flickered indiscriminately,
while mystifying calls have trailed
over our heads. Something small
and ten parts invisible shrilled

in the reeds in continuous protest,
presumably, at our unseeing trespass
till we feared for its taut, frantic heart.
Then we passed a stern-looking swan's nest

and coming along the path to the bridge
spotted an unmistakeable country pub
overlooking the river, and went in.
There we drank a good deal about the country

and said this was really the way
we ought to be spending every Saturday.
A river is a fine place for words
on a fine morning, and seeing things.

Quartet

I'd heard their youthful laughter
a quarter of an hour earlier
as they squeezed theatrically out
of a clapped-out Datsun Violet.

Now they're the festival quartet,
whom the vicar is pleased to welcome
on this their first visit,
taking a moment or two to relate

the story of the resident bats
who generally emerge from hiding
about eight o'clock, and may flicker
round the nave above our heads, the vicar

reveals, though they are harmless,
and make no noise. So, silent
as bats to come, we wait
for Haydn to emerge, anticipating

four or five movements will perhaps
pass unchallenged before the bats
begin. Which, mid-Mozart, they do;
on cue they come swerving

and jittering allegretto out of the dark
to give a performance of marked
bravura and silence, well above
our heads, till half-time.

We move towards the coffee or wine,
the mauvy sky, an easy moon
strumming along behind the pines,
and some musical conversation.

But there's unsuspected din
outside, a cacophony most un-
classically unrestrained,
and looking upwards it seems

as if every nob and nodule
of silhouetted stone's singing.
It's the performance continuing
theatrical; the whole cathedral's

thousand-strong backing of clamorous
seeming-carvings is — starlings,
assembled in shrill festival
to commemorate old Haydn's

raucous laughter, the arty battiness
of youth in ancient motors, vicars'
voices strumming, and above our heads
the clapped-out moon andante whitely rising.

Telemachus Leaving

It must have been always like this.
The light must have come as it does

this morning, shaping the mountains
that fall to the sea on our left,

giving them contour and shadow,
revealing isolated settlements,

smoke, small beaches, and boats
drawn up above high water.

It must always have been the same,
the clouds drawn up along Ithaca's

long spine, like a frail fleet
setting out hopefully, young men

escaping the island's stony
silences, leaving the mulish

obstinacies of field and terrace.
Somewhere there is remote news

of you, of whether you live,
whether after years on the barren

slopes of Ocean, you still dream
of sometime sailing into slack water

in Ithaca's small haven. Leaving,
I imagine you turning this headland,

feeling the responsive sea lifting
from its scintillant oily languor

to the thudding swell beyond Sami
and next those twisting sheer cliffs

coming nearer then falling behind,
the distant whitening under

the coiled rockface, the narrow
bay tempting us in. The sea

must always have been the way
we learned desire for the land's

inexhaustible stillnesses —
caves with vines shading

the entrance, oil poured
from deep long-stored jars,

the clear stream across the beach,
dark roots of olive-trees.

At sea we rehearse the land,
as respite, pause, drawn breath,

an end to being surrounded
by the endless claim of horizons.

Old Man in Greece

When it is my fate
or if it is
to reach about eighty

I should like
to shout in public a bit
like this old man

who waves his arms
at the other old man
stood in the road

or the road itself
which certainly merits
some mild

abuse. He sits
at a cafe table
between be-clouded

mountain and benign
sea at about 10-30am
without any visible

drink leaning
forward on a stick
trying a lyric

gravelly falsetto
on some meanderous
under-the-olive-tree

tune that drives
a green lizard up
round the other side

into the shade.
When he walks off
with a small laugh

and a shout waving
his stick at nothing
in particular

though four cats
shrink back under
a crumbless table

it must be a mild
rebuke directed at
lives that fail

to include at about
eighty humming
along a pot-holed

road by an old sea
that's being lyrical
in a quiet gravel-

voiced way, drawing
assurance from things
like skinny

cats un-clouding
mountains and waving
one's arms about.

In the Wine Section Again

My eyes drifting along the dark shelf
take a second or two to recognise
then credit the solemn downward gaze

of four swaying faces —
a clutch of swallows being reared
in the supermarket wine-section

that seem to be peering down
in a somewhat critical spirit
on what's already my second visit.

This astonishing quartet
is as worth gazing back gratefully at
as last night's Butari was,

especially bunched so tight up
that their mouths (for the instant closed)
join in a shaky smear of cheap

silver eye-brow pencil, their heads
still so bristling with soft spiky down
they look like the victims of reckless acupuncture.

They're waiting quietly and restlessly
for their parents who we discover
in the next instant's flinch of discomposure

zoom in and out of the shop entrance
as if we weren't there, staring us
in the face for a thousandth of a second

and threatening to gouge our shoulders,
though destined to keep missing
with the sort of unfailingly

reckless accuracy vouchsafed
to those the unerring gods guide.
Perhaps they're welcomed indoors

as bringing luck, or timeless skill,
and perhaps there's till some notion
drifting in the tolerant air

of this old island about living
closer or at least less shrinkingly
one species with another.

And when we're almost grazed
by something as graced as they are,
something quite arrowlike

that's also endlessly capable
of sidestepping itself like something
nipping round Hermes' ankles,

threading the edge of the harbour
as if mending the invisible ghostly nets
laid out there since before Homer;

when some thing just a bit divine
steps inside your front door
you remember. So, as on our

last evening we four too sway a little
in our transients' nest in the Villa
Tasos (c/o tonight Dionysos) where

they've already tried some empty rooms
and flutteringly, flatteringly, inspected
possible corners and niches,

I'm imagining that when we've gone
they might remember us, for our few human
moments of quiet stupefaction.

Robert Hull

Born in Lancashire and now living in Sussex, Robert Hull has been a school-teacher (Head of English) both in this country and in Canada, and a Consultant for the Open University. He holds two part-time lectureships, runs Writing Workshops for adults, and has edited several poetry anthologies for middle-school age children that have been published by Wayland. He is also the author of *Columbus* (Wayland, 1992) under the pseudonym of Roger Grimsby, and, under his own name, of two highly-acclaimed books about teaching: *The Language Gap* (Methuen, 1985), and *Behind the Poem* (Routledge, 1988)—a teacher's view of how children come to write and re-write poems and of how they make aesthetic choices in their writing. Robert Hull is a regular contributor to *Cumberland Poetry Review* (USA). Five of the poems in *Encouraging Shakespeare* appeared in *Peterloo Preview 2* (1990).